EPILEPSY

OTHER BOOKS BY THE SILVERSTEINS

Sleep and Dreams, Life in the Universe, Unusual Partners, Rats and Mice, The Origin of Life, The Respiratory System, A Star in the Sea, A World in a Drop of Water, Cells: Building Blocks of Life, Carl Linnaeus, Frederick Sanger, Germfree Life, Living Lights, Circulatory Systems, The Digestive System, Bionics, Harold Urey, Metamorphosis: The Magic Change, Mammals of the Sea, The Nervous System, The Sense Organs, The Endocrine System, The Reproductive System, The Code of Life, Guinea Pigs, The Long Voyage, The Muscular System, The Skeletal System, Cancer, The Skin, The Excretory System, Exploring the Brain, The Chemicals We Eat and Drink, Rabbits: All About Them, Animal Invaders, Hamsters: All About Them

EPILEPSY

Dr. Alvin Silverstein and Virginia B. Silverstein

With an Introduction by
J. Gordon Millichap, M.D., F.R.C.P.,
Consulting Editor

J. B. Lippincott Company
Philadelphia and New York

For permission to use the photographs on the following pages, the authors gratefully credit: John Ebling, *Amarillo News*, 57; Epilepsy Foundation of America, 54, 55, 56; Grass Instrument Company, Quincy, Mass., 21 (Model 8-10-10, 10 channel Electroencephalograph), 22, 24, 27; Jean Krulis, 20, 35, 48; National Institutes of Health Library of Medicine, 17; National Institute of Neurological Diseases and Stroke, 37; New York Public Library Picture Collection, 52; Roche Laboratories, Inc., Nutley, N.J., 38.

U.S. Library of Congress Cataloging in Publication Data

Silverstein, Alvin.
  Epilepsy.

  Includes index.
  SUMMARY: Describes the causes, symptoms, effects, and treatment of the various forms of epilepsy.
  1. Epilepsy—Juvenile literature. [1. Epilepsy] I. Silverstein, Virginia B., joint author. II. Title.
  RC372.S55   616.8'53   74-31382
  ISBN-0-397-31615-1   ISBN-0-397-31624-0 pbk.

FOR MORRIS AND HANNAH SILVERSTEIN

CONTENTS

INTRODUCTION

The sudden occurrence of a convulsion in a child is a terrifying thing to witness, particularly for a parent but also for a concerned friend or school teacher. "When will the convulsion stop?"; "Will the child recover?"; and, "What can I do to help?" are the immediate thoughts that flash to mind. In an adult epileptic, the spasmodic movements and distorted facial expression may be even more frightening and may conjure thoughts of insanity and contagious disease.

Dr. Alvin and Virginia Silverstein discuss epilepsy objectively, without emotional involvement or scientific bias. They have succeeded in writing in layman's terms about the history of epilepsy, the ancient misconceptions of the nature of the disorder, the modern scientific viewpoint, and the exciting medical discoveries that have led to the development of new and better treatments. The book is written primarily for young people, but teachers, parents, social workers, and the concerned layperson as well as patients will find it informative and interesting.

The management of the epileptic problem includes not only the control of the patient's seizures but also the education of his friends, parents, and the general public in a better understanding and acceptance of the disorder. The social stigma attached to the term "epilepsy" is fostered chiefly by ignorance. The J. B. Lippincott Company and the authors are to be congratulated for bringing the subject of epilepsy out of the closet and into the classroom and public library.

> J. Gordon Millichap, M.D., F.R.C.P.
> Pediatric Neurologist and
> Professor of Neurology and Pediatrics
> Northwestern University Medical School
> Chicago, Illinois

EPILEPSY: THE MISUNDERSTOOD DISEASE

The quiet of the classroom is broken by a sudden cry. A child topples from his seat to the floor. His body is strangely stiff. Then, as his classmates watch, his arms and legs begin to twitch and jerk. For a few minutes he lies there, thrashing wildly. Then he relaxes. His eyes blink sleepily. As his friends help him up, he murmurs confusedly. But soon he is back at work as though nothing had happened. Indeed, he may not even remember that anything did happen.

An epileptic seizure can be a frightening event, both to live through and to watch. It is not surprising that people hold perhaps more incorrect ideas about epilepsy than about any other disease. Some people think epileptics are crazy, or feebleminded—that epileptics should not be allowed to marry, to hold a job—that they cannot live any sort of normal life. Even people who do know something about this disease may feel upset if they see someone having a seizure. They may be unsure what, if anything, they can do to help.

Yet epilepsy is not a rare disease. It is thought that about 2 percent of the world's population suffers from some form of epilepsy—more than four million people in the United States alone. There are probably more epileptics in this country than all the Americans who suffer from cancer, tuberculosis, cerebral palsy, muscular dystrophy, and multiple sclerosis combined.

Modern medical research has discovered many effective methods of treating epilepsy. With antiepilepsy drugs, about half of all epileptics can be completely free of seizures, and many of the others can be greatly helped. But what epileptics need now more than anything else is understanding. Too often, epileptics are treated as though we were still living in the Dark Ages, when people with the "falling sickness" were thought to be possessed by evil spirits. Too often, an epileptic and his family are made to feel that the disease is something shameful that must be hidden.

In more than three-quarters of the cases, epilepsy begins during childhood or adolescence. These growing-up years are the most important in forming an individual's personality and developing the knowledge and skills that will be used in later life. If epileptic children meet constant prejudice and fear in the people around them, if they are treated as though they are somehow "peculiar" and are not allowed to take part in the normal activities and fun of life, they may not be able to grow up to be balanced, productive adults.

Prejudice and misunderstanding can deprive an adult epileptic of the chance to work and raise a family. It is estimated that about a quarter of all the employable epileptics are unemployed. Many of those who are employed are working at jobs that require far less than their full abilities.

It would be a real tragedy if, while medical science is providing the means for epileptics to live a full, satisfying life, prejudice and fear prevent them from doing so. We all need to know more about this misunderstood disease.

EPILEPSY IN HISTORY

The ancients believed that an epileptic was seized by a god or a demon who took possession of his mind and body and caused him to fall down writhing. Indeed, the modern term *epilepsy* comes from a Greek word meaning "seizure." Another name that was commonly used for epilepsy in ancient times was the "sacred disease." It is a popular thought today that epileptics were considered holy and that the confused mutterings they might utter just before or after an attack were treasured as inspired prophecy. But in fact the ancients more often regarded epileptics as unclean, objects of fear and disgust.

These ancient attitudes toward epilepsy are reflected in an incident in the Bible, related by Luke (9:37 ff.). A father with an epileptic son was in despair. The doctors of the village had been unable to help him. Even a specialist in the capital city, Jerusalem, could offer little hope. Then

Jesus of Nazareth entered the village. Holding his son by the hand, the father hastened to meet the famous miracle worker and poured out his story: "All at once a spirit seizes him, and he suddenly cries out, and it convulses him till he foams at the mouth, and it leaves him after a struggle badly bruised." No sooner had he said these words than the boy uttered a cry and fell to the dusty street. The people of the village backed away in fear. Jesus calmly rebuked the unclean spirit, and the boy recovered immediately. The crowd drifted away, but some of the villagers came close and spat on the boy as a way to prevent the evil spirit from attacking them too. (The practice was so common in ancient times that epilepsy was sometimes referred to as *morbus insputatus*, the "spitting disease.")

Epilepsy is probably the oldest known disease of the brain. It was mentioned in the laws of Hammurabi, the king of Babylonia, more than two thousand years before Christ. The disease was known to the ancient Egyptians and to the ancient Hebrews.

Even in the early days, there was a battle between the superstitions of the general public and the more scientific ideas of doctors, who had observed epilepsy more carefully. The great Greek physician Hippocrates wrote a book, *On the Sacred Disease*, in 400 B.C. In it he said, "The sacred disease appears to me to be no more divine nor more sacred than other diseases. . . . Men regard its nature and cause as divine from ignorance." Instead of believing that epilepsy is the result of a seizure by gods or demons, Hippocrates thought it to be a disease that begins in the brain and is often hereditary. Galen, another great Greek physician, who lived more than five hundred years later, also felt that epileptic attacks begin in the brain. He described the warning signs that often come just before an epileptic seizure and introduced the word *aura*, which is still used. (One of Galen's patients described his warning signs as "like a cold breeze," and the word *aura* originally meant "breeze.")

The views of these ancient physicians are quite similar to what is now known about epilepsy. But it was a long time before they were generally accepted. During the Middle Ages, there was a widespread belief that epileptic seizures were due to possession by demons. In the sixteenth and seventeenth centuries, most people believed firmly in Satan and his devils. Sometimes a distinction was made between the natural disease, epilepsy, and demonic possession, the effects of which might seem very similar. Physicians were called in to test the suspected patient. Sometimes epilepsy itself was thought to be caused by witchcraft.

Along with these superstitions, there were many other incorrect ideas about epilepsy. It was thought that the disease was contagious, and that anyone exposed to the breath of a person having a seizure could catch the disease. So epileptics were often treated like lepers, and special iso-

Pilgrimage of the Epileptics to the Church of Molenbeeck-St. Jean. *Engraved by Hondius, 1642, after Pieter Brueghel.*

lation hospitals were built for them. Another theory held that epilepsy was controlled by the moon. Treatments for epilepsy ranged from strange concoctions such as frog's liver, dog's blood, human urine, or peony juice, to applying hot irons to the head and even cutting a small hole in the skull (to allow the "mischievous matter" to escape).

Gradually the old superstitions faded away. As more was learned about the body, more precise observations of epilepsy were made. Several different kinds of seizures were described and studied. The first major advance toward real control of epileptic seizures occurred by accident. English physicians found that the sedative potassium bromide helped to eliminate epileptic seizures. The first report on the treatment of epilepsy with bromides was published in 1861 by Sir Samuel Wilks. In 1912, in Germany, Alfred Hauptmann began successfully treating epilepsy patients with barbiturates. Later, Dilantin and other new anticonvulsant drugs were discovered. Now the modern physician has a whole assortment of drugs to use, alone or in combinations carefully suited to each patient.

WHAT IS EPILEPSY?

Doctors today are inclined to think of epilepsy not as a single disease, but rather as a group of effects resulting from a disturbance in the brain's electrical activity. For some types of epilepsy the causes are known; for other types the causes remain a mystery.

It may seem strange to think of electricity in the brain. Actually, though, electricity is a normal part of the brain's activity. The human brain contains billions of microscopic, threadlike nerve cells, or *neurons*. A neuron has branches at each end. These branches link the neurons of the brain together into complex, three-dimensional net-works. Each neuron acts like a tiny storage battery. It builds up an electrical charge through reactions of the chemicals it contains. It can then discharge and pass the electrical impulse on to the next neurons in the chain.

Every time you smell a flower or say a word or move

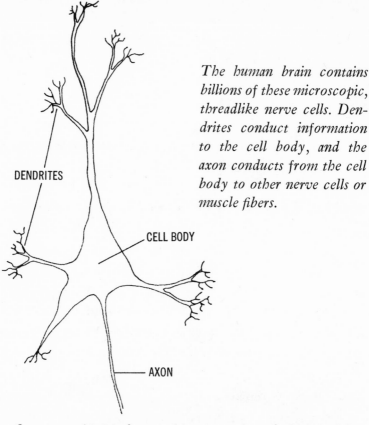

DENDRITES

CELL BODY

AXON

The human brain contains billions of these microscopic, threadlike nerve cells. Dendrites conduct information to the cell body, and the axon conducts from the cell body to other nerve cells or muscle fibers.

a finger or think of something, a series of electrical impulses races along a chain of neurons in your brain. At any moment, many electrical messages are flashing through various parts of your brain. Some of them report information from the eyes and ears and other sense organs. Others direct the movements of your body parts. Still others are involved in keeping the internal systems of the body running smoothly. And others take part in the constant stream of thoughts and imaginings that run through your mind. Like a busy switchboard operator, the brain normally keeps all these messages correctly sorted out and running simultaneously.

The constant electrical activity of the brain can even be detected at the outside of the head. If electrodes (metal wires or discs) are pasted to your scalp, a current flows through them. This current is very tiny—so tiny that it must be amplified (increased) many times before it can be recorded and measured. The machine that is used to pick up and record the electricity of the brain is called an *electroencephalograph* or EEG machine. (Its name comes

A patient having an EEG *made.*

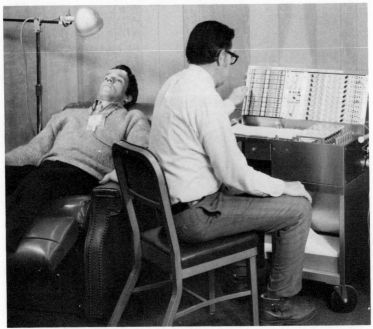

Photo by Fasch Studio

from words that mean "electric brain writing.") The recording it makes is called an *electroencephalogram* (EEG). An EEG is a series of squiggly lines drawn with moving pens on a long paper tape. There is one line for each of the electrodes attached to the head.

For a normal adult, the EEG shows a pattern of waves, about ten a second. But during an epileptic seizure, the EEG shows great bursts of energy, which come either much more or much less frequently than usual. A person who suffers from epilepsy usually shows an irregular EEG pattern even when he is not actually having a seizure.

During an epileptic seizure, there is a sort of electrical storm in the brain. Neurons become overactive and fire off

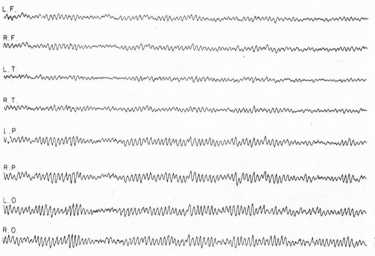

The EEG *of a normal adult.*

irregularly. The disturbance may spread to nearby neurons, jump to more distant ones, or race like wildfire through the whole brain. When this happens, all the brain's normal activities temporarily come to a halt. The person having a seizure may lose consciousness. His muscles may first go rigid and then begin contracting convulsively. He may even stop breathing. But soon the electrical storm in the brain quiets down. Most of the neurons begin working in harmony again. The seizure is over.

KINDS OF SEIZURES

Epilepsy may show itself in a number of different ways. The kind of seizure a person has is determined by where the electrical disturbance in the brain begins, where it spreads, and how fast it spreads. Generally each epileptic tends to have only one kind of seizure, but occasionally a patient has more than one type.

The commonest kind of epileptic seizure is called *grand mal* (pronounced "grahn mahl"), which literally means a "great illness." This is the kind of violent major attack that was described at the beginning of this book. The person suddenly loses consciousness. If he happens to be standing up at the time, he topples over in whatever direction he happens to be leaning. His body becomes as stiff as a board. He may give a sharp cry as air is forced

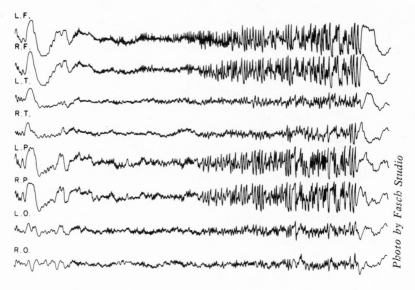

An EEG *taken during a grand mal seizure.*

through his voice box. Doctors call this part of the grand mal attack the *tonic phase*. The tonic rigidity soon passes and is replaced by a rapid jerking of all parts of the body. This is the *clonic phase* of the seizure. The person thrashes his arms and legs about and may bang his head on the floor. His jaws jerk, so that he may bite his tongue. A bloody foam collects around his mouth. His breathing is shallow or may seem to stop entirely. Often he may wet or soil himself. Gradually the jerking movements decrease and stop. The person lies limp. The convulsion is over.

A grand mal attack may last from less than a minute up to half an hour or more. If it is very brief, the person may be able to go back to his normal activities within a few minutes. But after a long seizure, the patient usually slips directly into a deep sleep or a coma. When he awakes, he may be weak and confused, restless and irritable. Nausea and vomiting, headaches, muscle soreness, and abnormal behavior may also follow such a seizure. These disturbances may last for only a moment or two, or they may persist for as long as a week.

Many epilepsy patients usually experience a period of warning signs, or aura, directly before an attack. The kind of sensations that make up the aura vary from person to person. Epilepsy patients have described auras including a tingling or numbness in various parts of the body, a pain in the abdomen, spots or colors before the eyes, a humming or buzzing sensation or a sound of music, headache, dizziness, peculiar tastes or odors, or just "a funny feeling." The aura is actually part of the seizure, as the electrical storm in the brain is beginning. The aura may be brief, but it may be long enough for the person to prepare for the attack—to make sure he is in a safe place, take off his glasses or false teeth, or do other things to help protect himself from possible injury.

A grand mal attack is frightening to watch, but actually the sufferer is not in any pain. Usually he is not in any real danger either, unless he is near something hard against which he may bang himself, or something like an electric heater on which he may burn himself. (While he is unconscious, he does not feel the heat or pain and cannot pull himself out of danger.)

Very rarely, a grand mal seizure can turn into a dangerous form of attack called *status epilepticus*. In this form, the storm in the brain does not quiet down. One seizure follows immediately after another, for hours or even days. If status epilepticus is allowed to continue, the brain is starved of oxygen. Brain damage or death may result. Status epilepticus is thus a great medical emergency, and a doctor should be called as quickly as possible if it occurs.

Another kind of seizure is so mild that family, friends, teachers, and even the person himself may not notice it. This is *petit mal* (pronounced "pe-tee′ mahl"—it means "little illness"). Some doctors refer to petit mal seizures as *absences*. The person having a seizure simply stops and stares off into space for a moment. He may blink his eyes rapidly or twitch his hands slightly. But often he seems only to be having a spell of daydreaming. Then he goes back to what he was doing as though nothing had happened. Petit mal attacks may occur as frequently as a hundred times in a day. They are commonest among children and may result in learning problems. Often the teacher does not realize the child suffers from petit mal and thinks he just isn't paying attention. In many patients, petit mal attacks tend to disappear as the child grows older. But in some patients, they may later be replaced by grand mal

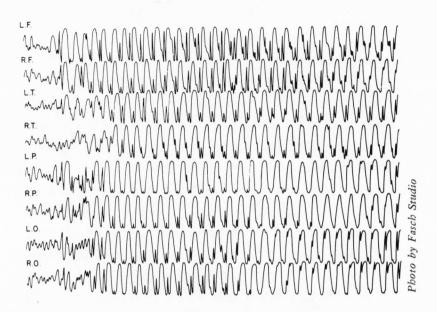

An EEG *taken during a petit mal seizure.*

attacks or other types of seizures. Thus, petit mal seizures should be treated promptly even if they seem to be only a minor inconvenience.

There are two other types of seizures that occur in young children. Both are often accompanied by mental retardation, and the attacks are difficult to control with medication. In one of these types, called *myoclonic spasms*, there is a sudden thrusting motion of the arms, while the body and sometimes the head jerk forward into a jacknife position. This condition occurs in infants and may be mistaken for colic. It is associated with a very abnormal EEG pattern. In the other type, called *drop* or *akinetic* attacks, all of the child's muscles suddenly go limp, and he falls to the ground. Then he generally picks himself up and goes back to whatever he was doing. (Young children who have this type of epilepsy may have to wear padded helmets to protect them from head injuries when they fall, many times a day.)

In *focal seizures*, the beginning of the abnormal electrical discharges can be traced to one small region, or focus, in the brain. One type of focal seizure is *Jacksonian epilepsy*. (It is named after Hughlings Jackson, an English doctor who made a detailed study of a case that occurred in his wife.) A Jacksonian seizure usually starts with a tingling sensation or a twitching in a finger or toe. The tingling or twitching "marches" upward along the limb as the electrical discharge in the brain spreads. The attack may die away after a few seconds or minutes, or it may spread farther and turn into a grand mal seizure. The person remains completely conscious until the actual grand mal attack.

A strange form of focal epilepsy is the *psychomotor seizure*. This form gets its name from the fact that the abnormal discharges act on both the mental processes ("psycho") and the muscles ("motor"). The patient may stop what he is doing and begin some automatic, repetitive movement, such as stroking his hair, rubbing his leg, or plucking at his clothes. He may make chewing movements with his mouth, or repeat short, senseless phrases over and over. During the seizure, the person is not unconscious, but he is in a sort of dream state. Afterward, he will remember little or nothing of what happened during the attack. Psychomotor epilepsy is often called *temporal lobe epilepsy*, because the focus is usually in one of the temporal lobes, the areas of the brain just above the ears.

CAUSES OF EPILEPSY

What causes the sudden abnormal bursts of electrical activity in the brain that result in an epileptic seizure? In some cases, the attacks can be traced to a specific injury to the brain. Perhaps there was an injury during birth, when the skull was still very soft. (The effects of such an injury may show up in early childhood, or not until many years later.) A gunshot wound may leave a scar that acts as an epileptic focus. A skull fracture in which a bit of bone presses on the brain can also cause epileptic seizures. So can certain diseases, such as *meningitis* (an inflammation of the membranes that surround the brain) and *encephalitis* (an inflammation of the brain itself). Brain tumors can also produce seizures. Cases that can be traced to a specific brain *lesion* (an injury or other variation from the normal) are usually referred to as *symptomatic epilepsy*. But for many cases, no apparent cause can be found. (This does not necessarily mean that there is not a specific cause, just that it has not been discovered.) Such cases are called *idiopathic epilepsy*. (The term means "cause unknown.")

There is a great deal of disagreement about how important heredity may be as a cause of epilepsy. It does play some role: epilepsy has been found to run in some families, and if one identical twin has epilepsy, the other twin is much more likely to have it also than are less closely related members of the family. Probably it is not epilepsy itself that is inherited but a tendency to react to damage to the brain with seizures. This idea is supported by two different observations: relatives of epileptics often have the same kind of abnormal EEG patterns, even though they never have seizures; and follow-up studies of soldiers with head wounds show that only one in four actually develops epileptic seizures.

The commonest causes of epilepsy vary with the age at which the disease first appears. In the first few years of life, birth injuries or brain defects that were present before birth can lead to seizures. Low blood calcium, low blood sugar, and hereditary conditions such as *phenylketonuria* (which also causes mental retardation if it is not detected and treated in time) can also produce seizures in infants and young children. *Febrile* (fever) *convulsions*, which occur in some babies during an illness, can be an indication of future problems. It has been found that about 5 percent of infants who have febrile convulsions will suffer from recurrent epileptic seizures in later child-hood. Idiopathic epilepsy usually does not appear until after five years of age.

In the growing child and adolescent, there are many important changes in the body chemistry, particularly in the hormones produced by the glands. These chemical changes can trigger epileptic seizures. For epilepsies that first appear in young adults, the leading causes are head injuries and tumors, as well as the delayed effects of birth injuries.

From middle age onward, brain tumors and blood vessel diseases, resulting in poor circulation to the brain, become increasingly important causes of epileptic seizures. But only a small fraction—perhaps 8 percent—of all cases of epilepsy begin this late in life.

EPILEPSY RESEARCH

Epilepsy still holds many mysteries. Researchers who are actively exploring this disease are searching for answers to two main questions: What causes epilepsy? How can it be better controlled and cured?

ANIMAL STUDIES

How do you test a brand-new drug? It may be effective, or it may not. It may be safe, or it may have unpleasant side effects; it may even be dangerous. In epilepsy, just as in other diseases, scientists generally try out promising new drugs on animals first. The most effective and safest drugs are then tried out in carefully controlled experiments on human patients.

In order to test an antiepilepsy drug on an animal, it

is necessary to produce epileptic seizures in the animal. It has been found that if an electric current is applied through an electrode implanted in a rat's brain, the animal will eventually have a convulsion. This never occurs during the first few days, no matter how strong the current is. It seems that the passage of electric current gradually changes the brain cells in some way, so that they begin to act abnormally, like the cells in an epileptic focus. Some parts of the brain seem to be more sensitive to electric current than others. A region called the *amygdala*, for example, deep within the temporal lobe, is especially sensitive; some other areas never spark seizures even if they are stimulated with electric current for two hundred days straight. Sometimes changes occur not only in the area right around the tip of the electrode, but also in another, distant region of the brain. A very similar effect is sometimes observed in humans with focal epilepsy; it is called a *mirror focus*. Researchers hope that studies with animals will not only provide convenient experimental conditions for testing new anticonvulsant drugs, but will also furnish clues to what causes epilepsy and how it can be prevented.

Another technique that produces seizures in animals is the application of tiny bits of chemicals directly onto the surface of the brain. Cobalt and aluminum hydroxide are two chemicals frequently used. Penicillin is the most effective seizure-producing drug, when applied directly to brain tissue. In one series of studies, researchers are testing the abilities of monkeys to remember and solve problems while they are having seizures produced by aluminum hydroxide. It has been found that monkeys treated with this chemical can remember past lessons just as well as untreated animals, but they have some difficulty learning new problems.

It has recently been found that baboons develop epileptic seizures if they are exposed to a rapidly flashing light. (Some human epileptics find that their seizures are brought on by a flashing or flickering light—perhaps even the flickering picture on a television set.) Various drugs were given to the baboons before they were exposed to the flash. Phenobarbital and Valium, two effective anti-epilepsy drugs, blocked the appearance of seizures. It is hoped that this technique may be used to discover new effective drugs.

EEG RESEARCH

The first reports on the human EEG were published in 1929 by Hans Berger. The early EEG researchers had to use a whole roomful of apparatus. But since then, advances in electronics have made it possible to reduce the whole EEG apparatus to a size little larger than a matchbox. It is hoped that small, portable EEG equipment that a patient can wear comfortably on his head as he goes about his

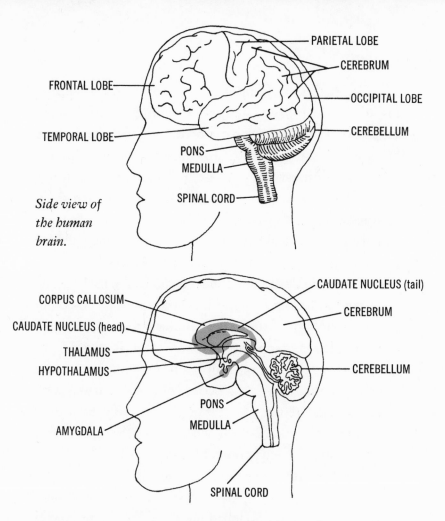

Side view of the human brain.

Outline drawing of the brain showing the approximate internal locations of regions within the cerebrum (shaded areas).

normal daily activities, broadcasting his brain waves to a remote recording device, will cast new light on the nature of the disease.

Computers are being used together with EEG apparatus in "depth electrode studies." Very fine electrode wires are inserted into various parts of the brain through small holes in the skull made by a neurosurgeon, and the patterns of electrical activity are recorded and analyzed. Electrodes only five microns across—about two ten-thousandths of an inch—have been used to record the electrical activity of individual neurons. In the area of the epileptic focus, it has been found that each neuron seems to be firing off at a high rate, quite independent of what is going on around it. In some cases of focal epilepsy that could not be controlled by drugs, such studies may permit the neurosurgeon to pinpoint the focus that is causing the trouble. If the diseased piece of brain is removed surgically in precisely the right area, a better control of seizures with medicines may result. (This type of surgery is used only for patients who have focal seizures that have not been helped by a prolonged period of medication.)

Another fascinating surgical method for treating severe, resistant cases of epilepsy is now being investigated. This procedure was developed on the basis of some animal studies on the effects of stimulation of the *cerebellum*, a part of the brain involved in balance and coordination of movement. Electrical current applied to the cerebellum seems to make seizure foci in the forebrain, or *cerebrum*, less apt to trigger an epileptic attack.

EEG apparatus is also being used in studies of the effects of epileptic discharges on behavior. In one study of children with petit mal, patients who showed a type of pattern called *spike and wave*, which is very easy to recognize on the EEG, were selected. The child, wearing electrodes, was asked to do various tasks. For example, a series of random numbers was read out loud, and the child had

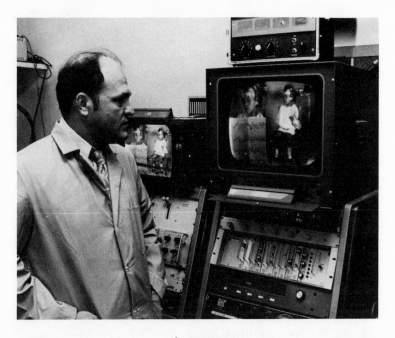

National Institute of Neurological Diseases and Stroke scientist demonstrates split-screen television equipment used in epilepsy research. One half of the screen shows a child performing various tasks while wearing portable EEG equipment. The other half shows the child's brain wave patterns.

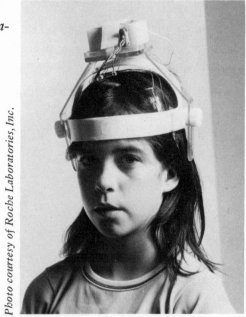

Child wearing porta-
ble EEG *equipment.*

to press a key every time he heard the number 6. Or he had to respond to a certain-colored light. The longer the burst of spike and wave, the longer the children took to react. But some were able to work on even while they were having a petit mal "spell."

In another series of studies, researchers found a relationship between petit mal seizures and the difficulty of the task epileptic children were asked to perform. By varying the difficulty of the task, it was possible to reduce the epileptic discharges to a minimum. Such studies may be very helpful in pointing out ways to teach epileptic children more effectively.

BIOFEEDBACK STUDIES

One of the most intriguing applications of EEG research has been the development of biofeedback machines. A person or animal is hooked up to an EEG machine with special attachments that give a sound or light signal each time the recordings show that he is producing a certain kind of brain wave pattern. For example, a pattern called *alpha waves* is produced when a person is relaxed and awake. With the aid of the "feedback" signals, he can learn to produce a particular kind of brain waves whenever he wants to. "Alpha feedback" is claimed to be very helpful in teaching people to relax. Techniques of biofeedback conditioning have also been used successfully to train people to lower their blood pressure and produce other desirable effects.

Similar techniques are being used to help control epileptic seizures. The first experiments were conducted on cats. It was found that cats produce a special rhythm of twelve to sixteen cycles when they are relaxed and not moving. This rhythm was named the SMR because it comes from a part of the brain called the *sensorimotor cortex*. When cats were trained to produce an unusually large amount of SMR, they were found to be resistant to drug-produced seizures.

Researchers then began work with epilepsy patients who had not been helped by drugs. Within a month of training, these patients were able to produce SMR at will. In three months there was a definite reduction in the number and severity of their seizures. Now scientists are exploring this technique further and trying to find out how biofeedback training controls epilepsy. At the moment it is very experimental and not a practical method of treatment for most patients with epilepsy.

BIOCHEMICAL STUDIES

Many researchers believe that the chemical balances of the brain and body may be key factors in epilepsy, as well as in other diseases. They hope that biochemical studies may provide a key to understanding the basic causes of epilepsy and suggest ways to cure it. In some of these studies, bits of brain tissue removed during operations on epilepsy patients are grown in an artificial fluid closely resembling the natural brain fluid and then are carefully analyzed and tested. In others, various chemical substances are determined in samples of blood or brain fluid of epilepsy patients. Already some very suggestive findings have been obtained.

Trace metals, for example, may play a role in abnormal electrical discharges in the brain. Children who chew on lead-containing paints and get lead in their bloodstream may suffer from convulsions. Some studies indicate that abnormal amounts of the trace metals zinc and copper may be involved in epileptic seizures.

One researcher believes that in epilepsy something goes wrong with the membranes that surround the nerve cells of the brain. Normally, sodium and potassium ions pass in and out of the cells in precisely controlled amounts. But a buildup of sodium ions inside the cells might spark them to discharge rapidly, leading to a seizure. The gas carbon dioxide is also involved in the electrical excitability of the nerve cells. Its concentration is controlled by an enzyme, *carbonic anhydrase*, which is normally found in the brain as well as in various other tissues. Without this enzyme, a seizure discharge cannot spread through the brain. A drug, *acetazolamide*, which destroys carbonic anhydrase, has been found to be helpful in controlling epilepsy in patients.

At the National Institute of Neurological Diseases and Stroke, it has been found that tissue from epileptic foci does not bind up as much of a chemical called *acetylcholine* as normal tissue. Acetylcholine acts as a *transmitter chemical*, that is, a chemical that passes nerve impulses along from one neuron to another. Perhaps the abnormal cells in an epileptic focus release acetylcholine too readily. Experiments on animals have shown that seizures result when too much acetylcholine accumulates around the nerve cells of the brain.

Biochemical studies are also pointing up some problems with the drugs used to control seizures and suggesting ways to improve the treatment of epilepsy. It has been found, for example, that patients who have been taking anticonvulsant medicines for a long time have low levels of certain vitamins, even if they have been eating a balanced diet. Reduced amounts of vitamin B_{12} and folic acid can produce anemia. Lowered levels of vitamin D can cause rickets in epileptic children who have been taking anticonvulsant drugs, although this happens very rarely. These patients need special vitamin supplements to keep them healthy.

OTHER RESEARCH

Studies of the families of people with epilepsy are helping to disclose the role of heredity in this disease. It has been found that some family members of epilepsy patients have the same kind of abnormal EEG patterns, even though they never have seizures. Some studies indicate that family members of epilepsy patients are more likely than the average to suffer from migraine headaches.

In one long-term program begun in 1956, sponsored by the National Institute of Neurological Diseases and Stroke, fifty-eight thousand mothers and their children have been carefully followed to determine the relationship between the events of pregnancy, birth, and the first month of life and the occurrence of epilepsy and other neurological disorders during childhood.

Other subjects that are being studied are the possible relationship between fever convulsions in infants and epilepsy in later life, and the question of whether there is a correlation between convulsions and brain damage and behavioral disorders. (It used to be thought that there was a special "epileptic personality," characterized as sly, suspicious, irritable, and so forth. But now it is realized that such unpleasant personality traits were generally the results of growing up surrounded by fear and prejudice, together with the constant uncertainty of not knowing when a seizure would occur. Doctors now feel that there is no special epileptic personality—people who suffer from seizures have the same range of personality characteristics as everyone else.)

LIVING WITH EPILEPSY

When a doctor gives a diagnosis of "epilepsy," the first reaction of the patient—or his parents—is usually fear and despair. He sees restrictions closing in on all sides— the prospect of loss of friends, of the kind of work he'd like to do. Yet today the opportunities for a person with epilepsy to lead an almost completely normal life are greater than ever before. And with greater understanding on the part of the people around him, the prospects can be even brighter.

CONTROLLING SEIZURES

One of the most troubling parts of life with epilepsy is the constant uncertainty. "When will the next seizure come? Where will I be, and what will I be doing at the

time?" A child with epilepsy, too young to really under-
stand how he is "different" from other children, may
awake from a seizure to find himself an object of ridicule.
For an adolescent, who often feels rather uncertain of
himself anyway, the possibility of embarrassment in front
of his friends may be particularly hard to bear. A seizure
in an adult may bring the threat of being fired from a job,
especially if his employer is not familiar with the facts
about epilepsy. So for the epileptic patient and his doctor,
the immediate and most important goal is to bring the
seizures under control, to decrease their number or eliminate them entirely.

When the patient has been thoroughly examined to
make sure there is no specific cause of the seizures, such as
a brain tumor, the doctor usually begins a program of
treatment with drugs. Drugs that are frequently used to
control grand mal seizures include phenobarbital, Dilantin,
and Mysoline. Petit mal responds to a different assortment
of drugs, including Diamox, Zarontin, and Tridione.
(Tridione was the first drug discovered that was effective
in petit mal.) Doctors are not entirely sure how anticonvulsant drugs work, but it is believed that they work on
the nerve cells *around* the abnormally discharging neurons
to make them less excitable; thus they help to keep the
electrical storm from spreading.

The particular drugs to be used in each case and the
doses that are most suitable for the patient have to be

worked out carefully. People differ in the way they ab-
sorb drugs into the bloodstream, use them in the body, and
excrete (eliminate) them. A method called *gas-liquid
chromatography* (GLC) is used to test for the exact levels
of anticonvulsant medicines in the blood.

Sometimes anticonvulsant drugs produce undesirable
side effects, such as drowsiness and confusion, dizziness,
skin rashes, and changes in the blood chemistry. Often
these side effects go away after a while, or they can be
eliminated by lowering the dose. Or it may be necessary
to switch to a different drug.

Once the proper combination of drugs is worked out,
about 50 percent of epilepsy patients can be completely
freed of seizures, and for another 30 to 35 percent the
number of seizures is greatly reduced. Usually the drugs
are taken two or three times a day, and the patient must be
very careful *never* to skip a dose. If he does, a seizure may
result. Indeed, if he stops the medication entirely, all at
once, he may go into status epilepticus. (An epilepsy patient going into the hospital for some other ailment should
always tell his doctors what anticonvulsant medications
he is taking, so that they can continue the drugs during his
stay.)

Must an epileptic continue to take pills all his life?
Some must, but others are able to stop the medication
eventually without having their seizures return. It has been
found that children often "outgrow" epilepsy. Their sei-

zures become less frequent as they grow older, and may even disappear. After a few years of control of seizures through drugs, the doctor may—slowly and carefully—decrease the doses. The patient may eventually be able to remain free of seizures without taking any medication.

For a few of those who are not helped by any of the drugs discovered so far, an operation may bring relief from seizures. The surgeon's aim is to remove the focus that is starting the electrical storms in the brain. Clues to the location of the epileptic focus may be provided by the EEG. The doctor may find other hints in a patient's description of the aura that comes before his seizures. If it is a particular smell, for example, the doctor knows that the seizure is beginning in a region of the brain involved in perceiving smells.

Dr. Wilder Penfield, a noted Canadian neurosurgeon, was the pioneer in the surgical treatment of epilepsy. His careful observations during operations have added much to our knowledge of the brain and how it works. Indeed, maps of the brain have been drawn up, in which specific parts or areas have been matched up with specific functions. Researchers know of vision centers, speech centers, hearing and smell areas, and so forth. Much of the brain mapping has been done during brain operations on epileptics. When an electrode stimulates a particular spot on the brain, the patient smells roses; when another spot is stimulated, he hears voices singing, or he sees the face of

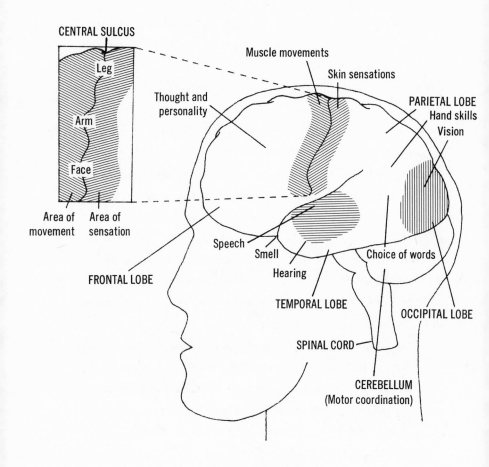

A map of the brain.

someone he once knew. All these sensations seem as real as though they were actually happening. (Curiously enough, the brain does not have any pain receptors. So operations on the brain can be performed with the patient wide-awake and chatting with the surgeon.) An epileptic focus may also be found during the operation, by stimulating various areas until the patient feels exactly the same as he does when he is about to have a seizure.

Drugs and surgery are not the whole story in controlling seizures. The patient's daily life can also have an important effect. It used to be thought that an epilepsy patient should be shielded from any possible stress. Doctors advised parents to take their children out of school and have them take long afternoon naps every day. Although some seizures may be sparked by stress or emotional upset, most patients who spent each day lying around resting got worse. Not only did they turn into chronic worriers, who felt sorry for themselves all the time, but they had *more* seizures than before. Now it is realized that a reasonable amount of healthy activity, both mental and physical, is good for epileptics and helps to reduce the number of their seizures. A common thought about epilepsy is, "What if a person had a seizure in the middle of the street, with traffic coming?" But many studies have shown that seizures almost never happen when the person is alert and active. They are much more likely to occur just after a nap, or even during sleep. (Some people, in fact, have seizures *only* while they are asleep.)

EPILEPSY AND INTELLIGENCE

Are epileptics less intelligent than other people? There are several reasons why many people have thought so. In the last century, before there were effective drugs for controlling seizures, epilepsy was an incurable disease. Epileptics were often sent to hospitals and homes to spend the rest of their lives—the same institutions that housed the mentally retarded and insane. After a while, people tended to think of epilepsy and mental retardation as being similar. This attitude was strengthened by the fact that the people in such institutions often received very poor care. They became depressed and withdrawn, and thus even the epileptics of normal intelligence would soon seem subnormal.

After effective treatments for epilepsy were discovered, there were some "scientific" studies that seemed to indicate that epileptics generally had low intelligence. But later researchers pointed out that all these studies were conducted on people in institutions, many of whom were *both* epileptic and mentally retarded. They did not take into consideration the many epileptics who were living reasonably normal lives outside the institutions, and especially those who were successfully hiding their condition from friends and neighbors.

It might seem logical to think that the recurring electrical storms in an epileptic's brain would damage the brain cells and make him grow less and less intelligent with each passing year. But studies of epileptic twins, each of whom had an identical twin who did not suffer from epilepsy, indicate that there is not usually any loss of intelligence. The twins of each pair were generally found to have just about the same i.q., even when one of them had been having seizures for years. It is known that everyone uses only a small fraction of his brain. Perhaps in epileptics, even if there is damage to some of the brain cells, there are plenty of undamaged cells to take over for them.

Indeed, there have been so many examples of epileptics who were unusually brilliant or gifted that it seems strange anyone ever thought of saying epileptics are generally unintelligent. The list of famous epileptics includes statesmen and rulers such as Alexander the Great, Julius Caesar, Alfred the Great, and William Pitt. (There has been much speculation on whether Napoleon Bonaparte had epileptic seizures; some present-day physicians believe he did, while others say he did not.) Religious leaders such as Buddha, Mohammed, and St. Paul are said to have had epilepsy. Great writers such as Byron, de Maupassant, and Dostoevski, and musical geniuses such as Handel, Berlioz, and Paganini were all epileptics. All these men were able to conquer or live with their disability and achieve great things. Plutarch, the Greek historian, wrote that Caesar did not use his headaches and seizures as an excuse to

Caesar did not use epilepsy as an excuse to pamper himself. This picture shows him crossing the Rubicon.

pamper himself. Instead, he tried to strengthen himself by long marches, a simple diet, and healthy outdoor living. The English writer Edward Lear had seizures nearly every day. (He marked each one with an X in his diary.) Yet he published seven very successful travel books and six books of humor and was a welcome guest in the noblest homes in England.

With people like these as examples, some researchers have even argued that epileptics as a rule tend to be *more* intelligent and gifted than other people. But it is generally thought that instead they show just about the same range of intelligence as everyone else.

LAWS RESTRICTING EPILEPTICS

At least since the time of the laws of Hammurabi in ancient Babylonia, many societies have had laws regulating what people suffering from epileptic seizures may or may not do. Some of the present-day laws are quite reasonable and sensible. For example, it would not be fair to permit someone who has recurrent seizures to endanger his own life and the lives of others by driving a car. But most states now do permit the licensing of epileptics who are under medication and have been free of seizures for a specified time (for example, at least one year).

But some of the laws restricting epileptics were based on mistaken ideas. Often the laws persisted long after the reasons for them had been discredited. For example, many states had laws permitting or even requiring that epileptics be sterilized to prevent them from transmitting their "tainted heredity" to the next generation. In some states, epileptics were not allowed to marry. Yet a war veteran, for example, who has epileptic seizures because of a head wound he suffered in the service could not pass on his epilepsy to his children. Even in idiopathic epilepsy, where people with the disease have a greater than average chance of having epileptic children, the risk still may be only a few percent. It has been a long, hard fight to get unfair laws such as these repealed. But now, in general, the question of marriage and a family is one for the individual

John Considine, TV actor and writer, has had epilepsy since he was a teenager.

epileptic to decide. Specialists in the medical field of *genetic counseling* can study the history of a patient's disease and family background and help to estimate the risk of passing on a tendency for epilepsy.

JOBS FOR EPILEPTICS

Economists begin to worry if our national unemployment rate rises as high as 6 percent. Yet it is estimated that among epileptics, as many as 25 percent are unemployed. And many who do have jobs are doing work that is far below the level of their true abilities. This is particularly sad because epileptics are healthier and have fewer seizures when they are doing full-time, challenging work.

Many employers refuse to hire epileptics because they are afraid that people who have seizures will have frequent accidents. Yet work experience has shown that this is not at all the case. Epileptics are employed in all types of work, from unskilled labor to the highest pro-

Garry Howatt, who plays with the New York Islanders, has had epilepsy since childhood and still takes medication.

fessional positions. In general, their accident record is as good as, or even better than the average.

In the 1950s, the U.S. Veterans Administration began an experimental workshop to determine whether epileptics could be helped by steady, paying work. The program was so successful that it grew into Epi-Hab U.S.A., Inc., a chain of workshops employing and training epileptics. Epi-Hab's safety record has been so good that it earned a 20 percent discount on its Workmen's Compensation Insurance. This was the case even though many seizures

Dawn Martin, an epileptic, was the 1969 Epilepsy Foundation of America poster child.

Steve Lamberson (on right), who has epilepsy, shown competing for his high school wrestling team.

have occurred during working hours. Epileptics, aware of their disability, tend to develop much more careful safety habits than the average worker.

Employers in private industry, impressed with the work done by Epi-Hab employees, have given jobs to many of them. Epi-Hab U.S.A., Inc., and other government and private agencies are continuing to give training and vocational counseling to epileptics and to urge employers to hire qualified epileptics.

EPILEPSY

WHAT TO DO IF A SEIZURE OCCURS

It is estimated that one person in every fifty may have epilepsy or a susceptibility to seizures. So there is a definite possibility that someone you know, or someone you may happen to be with, may have a major seizure sometime while you are present. What can you do to help? What should you do?

1. First of all, keep calm. There is nothing you can do to stop the attack once it has started. The person is not going to die. Except in the very rare cases when one seizure seems to follow another without the person's regaining consciousness, he does not need a doctor. There is no need to rush him to the hospital. (Imagine the embarrassment and expense an epileptic would have if he woke up in the hospital every time he had a seizure!) Usually the attack will be over in a few minutes. You don't have to worry about any danger to yourself—epileptic seizures aren't "catching."

2. Try to get the person into a position where he won't be in danger of hurting himself by knocking against something hard or sharp or hot, or by falling into water in which he might drown. But don't try to interfere with his jerking movements.

3. If you can do it gently, try to slip something soft, such as a folded handkerchief, between the person's teeth (from the side) to keep him from biting his tongue and

cheeks. Never try to force anything hard, such as a spoon, into the mouth of someone having a seizure.

4. Loosen any tight clothing, especially around the neck, and turn the person over onto his side, so that the excess saliva will drain out of his mouth.

5. Once the convulsive movements stop, let the person rest if he feels like it. Be very calm and matter-of-fact when you talk to him.

EPILEPSY TODAY

In past ages epileptics were often feared and scorned. Today, however, as scientists are learning more about the nature and causes of epilepsy, it is becoming more possible for epileptics to lead a full and normal life. In many cases, scientific advances have made it possible to control seizures, and continuing research offers the hope that someday we may achieve complete cures for epilepsy. Until then, what the epileptic needs most is sympathetic understanding from the people around him. He needs to be treated as a person, not as an object of fear. Progress is being made in this area, too. As more people learn the facts about epilepsy, the sufferers from this misunderstood disease are steadily gaining a better chance to be accepted and to live and grow to their full potential.

FOR FURTHER READING

Some helpful pamphlets about various aspects of epilepsy can be obtained by writing to:

> Epilepsy Foundation of America
> 1828 L Street, N.W.
> Washington, D.C. 20036

and

> Information Office
> National Institute of Neurological
>   Diseases and Stroke
> National Institutes of Health
> Bethesda, Maryland 20014

INDEX

Page numbers in italics refer to illustrations.

ALVIN SILVERSTEIN, born in New York City and raised in Brooklyn, developed an early interest in science. He received his B.A. from Brooklyn College, his M.A. from the University of Pennsylvania, and his Ph.D. from New York University. He is Professor of Biology at the Staten Island Community College of City University of New York.

VIRGINIA SILVERSTEIN grew up in Philadelphia and received her B.A. from the University of Pennsylvania. After her marriage, she worked as a free-lance translator of Russian scientific literature, doing extensive work for government and private agencies.

The Silversteins, who have collaborated on over thirty science books for young readers, live on a farm near Lebanon, New Jersey, with their six children.

DR. J. GORDON MILLICHAP is Professor of Neurology and Pediatrics at Northwestern University Medical School and is Pediatric Neurologist at Children's Memorial Hospital and Northwestern University Medical Center. From 1968 to 1973, he was Chairman of the Research Committee of the Epilepsy Foundation of America, and since 1966 he has been a member of the Epilepsy Foundation's Professional Advisory Board. Dr. Millichap received his medical training in England and is a Fellow of the Royal College of Physicians. He is the author of more than 150 contributions to the medical literature.

64